For Marie-Therese Pirotta – S.G.
For the good people of Chapel Allerton – S.A.

Text copyright © 2002 Sam Godwin
Illustrations copyright © 2002 Simone Abel
Volume copyright © 2002 Hodder Wayland

Series concept and design: Liz Black
Book design: Jane Hawkins
Commissioning Editor: Lisa Edwards
Editor: Katie Orchard
Science Consultant: Dr Carol Ballard

Published in Great Britain in 2002 as It All Makes Sense
by Hodder Wayland, an imprint of Hodder Children's Books

This paperback edition published in 2009 by Wayland,
an imprint of Hachette Children's Books,
338 Euston Road, London NW1 3BH
www.hachettelivre.co.uk

The right of Sam Godwin to be identified as the author
and the right of Simone Abel to be identified as the
illustrator of this Work has been asserted to them in
accordance with the Copyright, Designs and Patents Act 1988.

Cataloguing in publication data
  Godwin, Sam
  Making Sense of it All: a first look at the senses – (Little Bees)
  1. Senses and sensation – Pictorial works – Juvenile literature
  I. Title
  612.8

ISBN 978 07502 5882 1

Printed and bound in China

Making Sense of it All

A first look at the senses

buzzᶻᶻ

Making Sense of it All

A first look at the senses

Sam Godwin

WAYLAND

8

I like the sound of the bell, Mummy.

With our ears, we can hear all kinds of sounds —

Some sounds make us feel happy.

12

from loud, clanging noises...

Ding Dong! ding dong!

It didn't make me happy. It woke me up!

Zzzz...

... to soft, little whispers.

What is that rabbit doing, Mummy?

He has pricked up his ears to listen.

14

15

Our noses help us to pick up smells.

16

19

We taste food and drink with our tongues.

20

Some foods taste bitter. Some taste sour.

This tastes sour. Yuck!

And some taste sweet, or salty.

23

And some things feel cold or warm.

Brrr! This water feels very cold.

26

27

All about the senses

We use all our senses at once when we eat an apple:

We see the bright colour of the apple.

We feel the smooth skin with our fingers.

We taste the sweet flavour of the apple.

We smell the aroma as we peel the apple.

Useful Words

Aroma
A pleasant smell.

Bitter
A sharp, strong taste.

Nectar
A sugary substance made by plants to attract insects. Bees make honey from it.

Sour
An acid taste, like lemom or vinegar.

We hear ourselves chewing as we eat the apple. Yum, yum!